ALZHEIMER'S, MY MOTHER, AND ME

A Daughter's Memoir With Tips and Tools for Caregivers

Patti Bonczkowski

Diligence Publishing Company
Bloomfield, New Jersey

ALZHEIMER'S, MY MOTHER, AND ME

A Daughter's Memoir
With Tips and Tools for Caregivers

To contact Patti Bonczkowski to speak at your church, organization, seminar or conference
email: pattibonczkowski@yahoo.com

ALZHEIMER'S, MY MOTHER, AND ME

A Daughter's Memoir
With Tips and Tools for Caregivers

ISBN: 978-1-7331353-7-5

Printed in the United States

TABLE OF CONTENTS

DEDICATION 5

ACKNOWLEDGEMENTS 7

INTRODUCTION 9

CHAPTER 1 11

In The Beginning 11

CHAPTER 2 17

A Learning Experience 17

CHAPTER 3 21

It's Hereditary…Will I Get Alzheimer's 21

CHAPTER 4 25

Childhood Revisited... 25

CHAPTER 5 29

I'd Do It All Again... 29

CHAPTER 6 35

A Turn For The Worse... 35

CHAPTER 7 41

Life At Rehab.. 41

CHAPTER 8 45

Final Stop 45

CHAPTER 9 53

Abiding By Mom's Living Will 53

CHAPTER 10 59

Held By My Mother's Angel Wings.................................. 59

SONG: I Believe 64

CHAPTER 11 65

Reflections Of Love For My Mom 65

CHAPTER 12 71

My Alzheimer's Donation Page.. 71

CHAPTER 13 77

Tips And Tools To Make Your Life Easier 77

Alzheimer's Poem.. 86

CHAPTER 14 87

Pictures From Our Journey 87

ABOUT THE AUTHOR 99

ORDER INFORMATION 101

DEDICATION

This book is dedicated to my mother and BEST friend, Barbara Penny Bonczkowski, who has passed from Advanced Alzheimer's. You will be forever in my heart. Until we meet again. I love you Mom. Love your Patti-Cake.

ACKNOWLEDGEMENTS

I would like to acknowledge, all of the people who have been with me through my journey with my mom's Alzheimer's. I thank every one of you for all of your support through my living nightmare.

To my sister Pinky Aber, thank you for all of your love and support. I love you, Sis. To my aunt Paula Reinhardt (RIP), my uncle Frank, and my aunt Candy Otte, thank you for all of your generosity and support. I don't know where I'd be without you guys. I love you very much.

To all of my co-workers in CSP Dept. at the BCBSS, thank you for lending me your ear and always being there for me. I consider you guys my family.

To my mother's best friend, Annette Austin, you are an amazing person and friend. You were by my mother's side, even when she couldn't speak anymore. My mom always said, "I love Annette to pieces," and so do I.

To my significant other, Anthony Paletto, thank you for bearing with me while I wrote this book. I know deep in my heart, that my mom brought us together. I love you today and ALWAYS.

To all of the generous people, who have donated towards My Alzheimer's Walk for A Cure, I can't thank you enough.

To Linda (Landi) Vassilatos and Beverly Solimene, Maritza Panetta and Luz Morales, you guys are awesome, loyal friends. Thank you for everything. To Rosie Stolarz, I can't believe that we were reunited after 50 years. Miracles do happen. To EVERY friend in my life, I care about each and every one of you, and thank you for your friendship.

To Tisha Jones, thank you for inspiring me to finish writing my book.

To God, who has answered all of my prayers when I started losing faith. Thank you for restoring it.

To my dog, Precious Marie Bonczkowski, thank you for cuddling up next to me through all of my difficult days and nights, and going to visit Grandma at the nursing home and making her day too. Please give my mom a kiss for me. I really miss the both of you.

INTRODUCTION

In this book, I share my story with you and the knowledge that I have gained while taking care of my mom who had Alzheimer's. I was my mother's caregiver for quite a few years, and I have a lot of valuable information to share with each and every one of you.

I know that you will benefit from reading about my journey while I was taking care of my mom during her battle with Alzheimer's. I have also provided tips, tools and resources throughout the book that will help you in your or your loved one's personal fight against Alzheimer's

CHAPTER 1

In The Beginning

One year before my mom was stricken with Alzheimer's, she had asked me to go with her to an Elderly Law Attorney. She wanted me to become her Power of Attorney and Healthcare Representative, and she also wanted to do a Living Will in the event that my dad passed before her since my father was terminally ill. He passed in "2011" and my mom passed away in "2013."

After we left the attorney, we went to my parent's bank, because my mom also wanted my name on hers and my father's checking account. About a year later, my mom's memory was starting to fail, plus she was working two jobs. So I asked her if she'd like me to take over doing her bills, because I knew how busy she was. She gladly said yes. I noticed there was $10,000 overdrawn on her checking account, that deposits were not being recorded in the book, and lots of check numbers were missing.

My father never did the bills, so he couldn't answer any questions that I had regarding any transactions. I asked my mom, "Does the spa that you belong to take money directly out of your checking account, or do you pay them directly?"

She only replied, "YES."

I then asked her, "Do your employers hand you a check, or do they direct deposit it?"

She replied, "YES" again.

So I went down to the bank to go over her account with them.

The nightmare all began when my mother called me at work hysterically crying. All she kept saying was, "I can't, I can't!" Then she hung up the phone.

I called back and asked her, "What's the matter, Mom?"

She responded that she couldn't go back to work, that they demoted her and gave her an idiot's job working on an elevator.

I was at work, which was one and a half hours away from her house, and the only words that came out of my mouth were, "You don't have to go back there. Don't worry about anything."

I almost threw up. The thoughts kept going through my head, *"My father is terminally ill, and now my mom isn't going back to work."*

That's when I decided to cash in the $9,000 from my CD account and deposit the funds in my parent's account. Plus, my mother's aunt Betty had left my mom a small inheritance. Now at least they would have sufficient money in their checking account.

After my mom and I hung up, I proceeded to call her supervisor at the nursing home where my mother had worked. As I dialed the phone, I was thinking, *"We're in the twentieth century; there are no more elevator operators."*

Her supervisor explained to me that my mother had Alzheimer's. She said that she's worked around a lot of patients with my mom's condition, and the only reason she gave her the elevator job was because my mother used to be a very good worker. She liked her and didn't have the heart to fire my mom.

My mother worked at a nursing home in Sussex County. Her job was to update patient's charts for the doctors. I know it was a lot more involved than that, but I don't recall everything.

Now, it didn't matter. My mother's boss suspected that my mother had Alzheimer's!

I then took my mother to a neurologist. He asked her a lot of simple questions that she wasn't able to answer. He asked her address, phone number, and county that she lived in; when suddenly she got so frustrated with the questions and told the doctor that she knew that she was stupid.

The neurologist said that my mom had symptoms of Alzheimer's, but only an MRI could confirm his results.

My mother's era did not believe in going to doctors. She was born in 1934, and they didn't have technology like we have today. Back in her days, if you went into the hospital, you never came out alive.

The day of my mother's MRI, she was beyond furious that she had to go for tests. She kept slamming all of the cabinet doors, drawers, and the door to every room, until thank God, we had to leave. Not only was I getting a migraine from my mother slamming everything in sight, but I really felt bad for her.

My mother did not say one word to me on the way to the imaging center. When we arrived, I asked if she'd like me to come in with her, and she told me to just stay away. I was so hurt, because I wanted to console her and now I couldn't.

When my mom came out of the MRI, I asked her if she wanted to go get something to eat and look around this pharmacy that sold gorgeous things.

Her face just lit up with a huge smile and she replied, "Okay."

I can't recall how long it took, but it wasn't too long before the doctor called me with the results. It was confirmed. My mother definitely had Alzheimer's.

CAREGIVER'S TIP

You must take your loved one to the
doctor to confirm if they have Alzheimer's.
My mother's boss suspected that my
mother had Alzheimer's. I took my mother
to a neurologist. He asked her a lot of
simple questions that she wasn't able to
answer. The neurologist said that my
mom had symptoms of Alzheimer's, but
only an MRI could confirm his results.

Patti Bonczkowski

CHAPTER 2

A Learning Experience

The neurologist put my mom on Namenda to sharpen her memory. I honestly didn't notice anything different.

I started reading up on my mother's diagnosis on the Alzheimer's site. I read that you could take Namenda and an Exelon patch together. I inquired with her neurologist, and he gave me the prescription for the patch. More FALSE hope.

My mother cracked me up. One day, I saw her rubbing her back against the door frame. I asked, "Mom, what are you doing?"

She laughed.

I thought that maybe a tag was making her itch, so I went over to check out the situation. She was trying to get the Exelon patch off.

I also read that Aricept could help slow down the Alzheimer's. **Again, FALSE hope!**

I became heavily involved with learning about my mom's illness. I read weekly newsletters on the Alzheimer's site, started doing the Alzheimer's Walks where I've raised anywhere from $1,500 to $2,850 towards *"A Cure for Alzheimer's."* I've done research on new medications and purchased a book that I **strongly recommend** for all caregivers entitled, *"The 36-Hour Day"* by Nancy Mace. They call that book, the Alzheimer's Bible.

It's so scary. Most of the females on my mother's side of the family came down with Alzheimer's. (My great grandmother, my grandmother, my grandmother's two sisters, two second cousins and MY Mom).

I read an article about how to prevent Alzheimer's by doing puzzles, crossword puzzles and other activities to sharpen your mind. I became furious one day and called the Alzheimer's Association. I told them that doing all of those brain exercises might work for an elderly person, but it won't stop Alzheimer's. Scientists, presidents, and more influential people get Alzheimer's, and they do A LOT of reading and much more. The lady on the other end of the phone agreed with me.

Many years later, after my mom had passed, I read something that finally made some sense. Plaque build-up on the brain. Sticky plaques begin forming on a person with Alzheimer's brain, damaging nearby cells. For decades, doctors have sought ways to clear out these plaques, as a way to prevent or treat the disease. Many people build-up amyloid plaque and can't get rid of it. As of "2020," no treatment exists to prevent or delay the onset of Alzheimer's.

If you know someone with an early onset of Alzheimer's, have them tested and sign them up for clinical studies. There is **NO** cure for Alzheimer's, so going for a clinical study can't hurt.

CHAPTER 3

It's Hereditary...Will I Get Alzheimer's

I can vouch, from the evidence of my own family's history along with the findings from my research, that Alzheimer's is hereditary. This is especially true for females, but it does not mean that every single family member will get it.

I was always petrified of being tested for Alzheimer's because there is NO cure as of yet. The disease usually passes through the mother's genes, not the father's.

I know that people with strong religious beliefs will not like my next statement, but I cannot go through what my mom and the rest of my relatives on her side of the family went through.

I learned that Oregon has the Death with Dignity Act. This Act allows the terminally ill to end their lives through voluntary, self-administration of a lethal dose of medication prescribed by a physician for that intention.

Armed with that information and armed with the option of going to Oregon if I chose that route, I decided to go to a neurologist to see if I was carrying the gene.

The only downfall with the Death with Dignity Act is that you lose your life insurance benefits. Even though you're terminally ill, it's still considered suicide, and your beneficiaries will not get a penny. I've contacted my life insurance company, and that's basically what they told me.

The test that I took at my neurologist's office was called an EEG. Small metal discs (similar to an EKG), are placed on your scalp to show electrical activity of the brain. I was told to sit on this recliner, in a tiny pitch-black room, with a nurse sitting across from me. The goal is to hope that you fall asleep. If you do, the results of the EEG are greater.

The room was extremely dark, and I was able to fall asleep. With this test, they can't give you any sedatives to make you drowsy, because you'll be numbing the area that they have to read.

The good news is that I am not carrying the gene, but there are chances that I could still possibly get Alzheimer's because anyone can get it even if they are not carrying the gene.

CAREGIVER'S TIP

I was always petrified of being tested for Alzheimer's because there is NO cure as of yet. The disease usually passes through the mother's genes, not the father's.

Patti Bonczkowski

CHAPTER 4

Childhood Revisited

Alzheimer's made my mother into a child again. She lived almost an hour away from me, and I'd stay with her and my dad every weekend from Friday to Sunday night.

When I'd walk into my parent's house, my mom would clap, laugh, and say, "We're going bye-bye. Right Patti-Cake? We're going to go bye-bye. Right Patti-Cake."

My parents called me Patti-Cake my entire life. My mom was still living with my dad, but he was terminally ill. He had colon cancer, a weak heart, and blood clots all over his body from years of smoking, and he needed a new hip.

My father was so sick that he wasn't allowed to take pain killers, have chemo or have any more surgeries.

I was able to call to check on my parents every day, but my mom no longer knew how to answer the phone. When the phone rang, she'd walk around in circles and then finally hand the receiver to my father.

I knew that my mom was able to recognize people and read a sign, so I purchased a phone and put my picture and name on one of the large push button dials. Then I programmed my phone number where my picture was.

I tried over and over to tell my mother to press my picture whenever she wanted to speak with me. Before she was stricken with Alzheimer's, we'd call each other at least five times a day. Unfortunately, my mother couldn't comprehend how to use the button. She did happen to push the button, but when it rang, she handed me the phone.

My mom loved going to the Dollar Store, so every weekend, I'd take her there. She'd sing the entire way, "We're going to the Dollar Store, the Dollar Store," over and over; then she'd laugh because we were going out.

We used to take pretty long walks around the pond by her house and then go out for something to eat.

My dad (who as I mentioned earlier was terminally ill) got worse and ended up in the hospital, so I took my mom back home to live with me.

On the way to my place, we stopped at Walmart. I purchased my mom a raised toilet seat, a portable plastic bathtub rail, and Depends (in the event of an accident). I also went to a medical pharmacy and bought her a seat that acts like a Lazy Susan. You place the seat on your kitchen or dining room chair, have the person sit on it, then you gently turn the person to face the table.

While I was pushing my mother around Walmart in her wheelchair, I stopped to ask two-salespeople where something was. All of a sudden, my mom started screaming at the top of her lungs, which meant that she had to go to the bathroom. She kept screaming and screaming, until I was able to ask which way was the bathroom.

CAREGIVER'S TIP

I bought my mother a seat that acts
like a Lazy Susan. You place the seat
on your kitchen or dining room chair,
have the person sit on it, then you
gently turn the person to face the table.

Patti Bonczkowski

CHAPTER 5

I'd Do It All Again

It was extremely difficult being home and caring for my mom 24/7, all by myself. But as God is my witness, I'd do it all again for my mom.

I always prayed to God to help me find a way to take care of my mother when my dad got too sick or passed away. I needed to be there for my mom.

Everything worked out perfectly. I only had one bedroom with a full-size bed; I had just gotten out of a 29-year, live-in relationship and was laid off from a job that I was at for nine-years.

It was a blessing in disguise the way everything fell into place. I needed the room for my mother. I also needed to be home to take care of her and wanted her lying next to me in bed.

I figured having my mom next to me, that I'd feel her get out of bed, and I'd get up to make sure that she didn't lose her balance and fall. That is

NOT what happened at all. I was so drained from taking care of her all day that when I finally went to bed, I was out cold.

I would wake up and find my mom's Depends on the bedroom floor, and my mom would be sitting on my living room table, waiting for me to wake up.

During the course of the day, I'd wake up and take a quick shower, in the event that my mother would get out of bed. Then I'd get dressed and try to wake my mom up. I realized after a few days, that my mother did not want to get up until 12:00 noon.

The first few days when I woke her, she grabbed hold of my clothes and wouldn't let go. So I got to the point of letting her sleep until 12:00. This way, I was able to do bills and eat and clean our place.

Breakfast the first few days was a real learning experience for me. I'd sit her down at the dining room table, then I would prepare breakfast and tea for both of us. She would spit her food across the table, and a lot of the time it ended up in my tea or food. I learned to feed her after I asked her if she was hungry. When she was hungry, she'd reply, "yes" with a chuckle.

I had a real tough time trying to pick my mom up while she was sitting on the dining room chair, in order to face her towards the table. I finally solved that problem with the Lazy Suzan chair pad that I spoke of earlier, that you use by placing the person sideways on the chair, and then turning them gently to face the table.

I had to go down to Social Security with my Power of Attorney paperwork to become Representative Payee of my mother's account. To anyone who does this, make sure that you keep every receipt – in the event that you're audited. I used my mother's money strictly on Depends, clothing, medications and other things. I wrote on every receipt, the things that I purchased for her.

Daily routines were extremely exhausting. I'd wake up, take my shower, get dressed quickly, make my breakfast, do the bills, clean the place, literally struggle to get my mother out of bed, walk her into the bathroom so that she could go, then wash, dress, and feed her. You think it's difficult to dress a kid? Think of a dead weight adult. Now that's difficult!

I used to be able to give my mother a shower and wipe her when she got off of the toilet. I did this for years. Then one day a switch turned on in her mind, that said she didn't want me to help her in this area anymore. When I tried to help her from this point on, she'd push me hard to get away and would hurt me for going near her.

On the other hand, if I helped my mother onto the recliner to watch television, she was very content and happy. Just no more hygiene!

My sister and aunt were at my place together visiting one day. The three of us tried to get my mom off of the toilet, and she almost took all of us down. They didn't realize what I did on a daily basis, until they actually saw it.

If I had to go to the store for just milk or to pick up a prescription, I would have to go through my entire routine in the morning, plus follow behind my mother going up the stairs, hold under her arm on the way to my vehicle, get a good grip on her as I lowered her into the car, put her seatbelt on, go to the store, take her seatbelt off, go around to her side of the car, pull with all of my might to get her out, hold her under her arm again so that she didn't lose her balance, and ditto on the way back home. It was VERY exhausting, just to get one item at the store.

My mom was a happy go lucky person. When she came to live with me in September, I decorated for Christmas with all of my fiber optic snowmen, Christmas tree and Santa Claus. My mother would just sit in the recliner and admire all of the fiber optics.

I think that we saw the movie, *"What About Bob?"* at least 100 times. She would laugh hysterically every time that the psychiatrist got hurt. When the DVD ended, I placed it back into the DVD player, so that she could watch it again. For those of you who never saw the movie, it's pretty funny. Richard Dreyfuss and Bill Murray are two of the main actors.

CAREGIVER'S TIP

I had to go down to Social Security with my Power of Attorney paperwork to become Representative Payee on my mothers' account. To anyone who does this, make sure that you keep every receipt – in the event that you are audited.

Patti Bonczkowski

CHAPTER 6

A Turn For The Worse

One day, I became so TOTALLY drained from taking care of my mom 24/7, that I called an agency to send someone to my place to help me. I asked them to send over an aid just for 3 hours. When the aid arrived, I instructed her to just sit with my mom while I go to sleep. I had already bathed her, combed her hair and made breakfast. I just desperately needed sleep. I got enough needed rest that day and was able to build my strength up a little to continue taking care of my mom.

My mother didn't intake a lot of water, so every two weeks I'd have to bring her to Hackensack Hospital. My mother refused taking antibiotics or any other pill or liquid, so we would spend 14 hours each time in the emergency room.

One time, they had to admit my mom for four days. I slept next to her for 22 hours a day on a hard chair. Then I'd go home for two hours to take a quick shower and feed my dog.

On the third day, since I was a volunteer with the American Red Cross Disaster Team on a national level, they sent somebody to the hospital to bring me a cot.

I was scared to leave my mother because she couldn't speak, and only I was able to read her facial expressions.

As my mom's Alzheimer's advanced, her hygiene got worse. She was not wiping herself and didn't want to take a shower anymore. I was beside myself.

One morning, both of us woke up really sick with the runs, and I was beyond tired. It's not easy taking care of a person with Alzheimer's all by yourself.

I made an appointment at the doctor's office, for both of us. My mom had just gone to the bathroom again, and she really needed to be wiped. She refused to allow me near her, but I couldn't bring her to the doctor's without cleaning her first. So I figured that I'd put her into the shower and wash her good.

My mom turned her backside towards the wall of the shower. I was hoping that the water would hit the area that needed to be cleaned, so that when I dried her with a towel, I could wipe her dry.

Since my mother kept her back from me, I put on the cold water only so that she'd move towards me and I'd be able to clean her, which I used as a last resort and I've regretted it ever since. Unfortunately, that did not work.

When my mom got out of the tub, I went to wipe her behind really quick, but that only made her VERY frustrated.

She scratched me really hard across my chest and pushed me away with all of her might, then she stepped backwards and fell over the bathtub. I went to grab her, but she was still soaking wet from not allowing me to dry her.

When she went over the tub backwards, she hit her head on the tiled walls, then proceeded to fall down into the shower and hit her head on the tub.

My mom laid there saying over and over, "Help me. Help me."

I ran and got a blanket to place over her. I got my portable heater to put on the edge of the tub to keep her warm (No water was in the tub), then I called 911 immediately.

The cops took down a report, and the ambulance took my mom to Hackensack Hospital, where again I slept by her side every day.

A social worker came in to speak with me to inform me that they were releasing my mother that day. She also instructed me to make plans as to where I wanted my mother to go, because she couldn't go home with me.

My head wasn't processing that my mother was being released, and I could not take her home with me. I asked the social worker to come back later.

I called one of my friends and asked her to look up Alzheimer's rehab/nursing homes. I picked one that was in Westwood, New Jersey, which I didn't realize at the time was 40 minutes from where I lived.

The night before my mother was to be released from the hospital, we had a blizzard. I only had a small vehicle, and there was no way that I'd be able to follow the ambulance, or even get a chance to see the place where she was being admitted.

Even though my mother could not speak anymore, until the day that she passed away, she understood every word that I said to her.

I sat down beside her, trying very hard not to cry, but I felt the tears swelling in my eyes. I explained that an ambulance was coming to pick her up, and that I was not able to go with her. I promised that I'd be there when she woke up in the morning.

With that, she started to cry really loud. I could not bear to watch them take away my mother. I ran into the bathroom and closed the door behind me. I was crying hysterically in the bathroom, and my mom was crying really loud as they took her out of the room. I was praying that it was only a nightmare, but unfortunately, it wasn't.

CAREGIVER'S TIP

It's okay to ask for help. One day, I became so TOTALLY drained from taking care of my mom 24/7, that I called an agency to send someone to my place to help me. I asked them to send over an aid just for 3 hours. When the aid arrived, I instructed her to just sit with my mom while I go to sleep.

Patti Bonczkowski

CHAPTER 7

Life At Rehab

The following morning, I got up very early to see where the ambulance had taken my precious mother.

I never liked being away from my mother, because I was the only person who could read her expressions and know what she wanted.

The roads were drivable the following day, with the exceptions of side streets. I found the rehab/nursing home with no problem. As time went by, I went about the business of getting my mom settled in. The rehab/nursing home had a gorgeous dining room area, where I always took my mom to eat.

One day, my mom and I were watching television when all of a sudden, she started laughing really hard. I asked her what she was laughing at, and she just kept laughing. Now I was checking her up and down, because I knew that she had to have done something bad, but I wasn't sure what it was. Finally, I looked at her IV machine and noticed that she yanked the IV out of her arm. I asked her, "Did you do that?"

She replied, "yes" and started laughing again.

I'd leave my home every day by 8:00 a.m. to go to the rehab/nursing home, and I'd get back home by midnight. I made sure that I fed my mom breakfast, lunch, and dinner, and I'd take her to the many activities that they had at the home.

My mother went to every function at the rehab/nursing home, even though she couldn't comprehend what was going on. They had movie night, horse races (with large cardboard horses), Bingo, and a few other things.

When the patients at the rehab/nursing home won, they received fake money that they used at the end of the month, to purchase donated stuff on the table. For example, my mom could choose, nail polish, a brush, a stuffed toy, perfume or other odds and ends.

It was so cute, because my mother still knew the word MONEY. When she won, she'd hold the money in her hands and just laugh. When she received her fake money, I would tell her that I'd take her to Baskin-Robbins with her money later on that day. Then she'd laugh real hard. Baskin-Robbins was next door to the rehab/nursing home, which I took my mom there a few times a week.

My mother had to go to rehab sessions every day. The first few days, I looked through the window, so that I would not distract her. After about a-week, I went in to watch how she reacted to each exercise.

They had my mother hit a balloon with a fly swatter, which made her laugh. As I watched my mother go through her sessions in rehab, I noticed that some of the exercises were causing her a lot of pain. After about the second or third day of watching her in pain with certain exercises, I told them that they were making her worse, in which they agreed and stopped her treatments.

Being that my mom was no longer going to rehab, the nursing home informed me that they had no room in their nursing home for any more patients and that I'd have to find another nursing home right away.

I was staying with my mother at least 16 hours a day. I did not own a computer, and the cell phones back then did not have text or internet. There I was, all alone with no guidance what-so-ever. I cried every night, and even when I pulled up to the nursing home. Everything was taking a toll on me. I just wanted to protect my mother, 24/7, but they were not allowing it.

I begged God to please help me, and I started losing faith. Then suddenly, my prayers were answered and my faith was restored.

It killed me, but I did not go to see my mother during the day. I had to look for a permanent nursing facility that could take my mother in less than a week!

CHAPTER 8

Final Stop

The next day I went to two-nursing homes in Bergen County, but they didn't do anything for me. I knew that I wanted a nursing home with an Alzheimer's unit, so that my mom would get better care being that they dealt with people like her.

I came across a nursing home in Clifton, which I was very impressed with. The place was immaculate and had an Alzheimer's unit. There were no rugs on the floor that smelled like urine, plus they gave my mother a private room.

Shopping time – I went out and bought beautiful towels to hang in my mom's private bathroom, and a bunch of Nemo's (fish) with suction cups. I placed Nemo all over the bathroom walls. Every time my mother went to the bathroom, she'd point at each and every one of them and say, "Nemo, Nemo, Nemo." Then she would laugh.

The nursing home had two dining areas, but after all of the patients ate, they'd all return to a glass-enclosed room so that the nurses and staff could observe them.

Both dining rooms had a VCR and television. So when the patients went to the glass-enclosed room, I took my mother to the really nice dining room to let her watch "*What About Bob?*"

I bought my mother a boom box to play cassettes on. She loved the nursery songs; *London Bridges Falling Down, Ring Around the Rosie* and others.

I was able to bring my mother anywhere that I wanted to within the nursing home and their courtyard. Most of the floors had fish tanks, and we went to see every one of them. We'd also go to another room that had a lot of tiny finches (birds). My mother really enjoyed watching the fish swim around and the birds flying and chirping.

Being that I was at the nursing home all day and night, I learned to change my mother and her bedding. The nurses and aids everywhere are really understaffed so I figured that I'd take care of my mother while I was there.

I'd roll her onto her side, remove part of the sheet, then roll her onto her other side and remove the rest of the sheet. Then I'd do the same routine while placing new sheets on her bed.

I spent long hours at the nursing home until I saw that my mom was changed, had her pain medication and had fallen fast asleep. Some nights I'd leave at midnight, because she was still wide awake.

My mother's right hand became deformed, and her nails started digging into her hand. When that happens, it means that the left side of the brain has died. Or at least, that's how it was explained to me. The left side of the brain is responsible, for controlling the right side of the body.

I tried very hard to open my mother's hand, but it was like rigor mortis had set in. I asked the nurse what I could do to prevent my mother's nails from cutting into her hand, and she told me they could order a Posey terry cloth covered palm cone.

When it arrived, I had to pry my mother's hand open, place the palm cone in her palm, and release her fingers. That was the perfect solution.

Finally, after two years of being unemployed, I was offered a part time position with the county, and all I kept thinking about was my mom. I was a nervous wreck, not knowing if she ate, had a dirty diaper, or not knowing how she was feeling that day.

I had finally started working which was great, because I had received three eviction notices from my landlord. I was laid off from my job prior to that, then my mother came to live with me, and my only concern after that had been my mother.

Luck was with me again with this new job offer. I was offered a part-time position, from 9:00 a.m. to 2:00 p.m., which meant that I was still able to spend quality time with my mom and feed her dinner.

The nursing home was a half hour away from my job, and I was still able to stay with my mother until she fell asleep, making sure that she had her medication, and was dry.

I was excited to have a job, but that meant that I couldn't be with my mom all day and night. I had promised my mother that I would never place her in a nursing home, but I wasn't given a choice. Since she fell in the bathtub and was in constant pain afterwards, they would not allow me to take her home with me.

One day when I went to visit with her after work, I noticed that my mother's feet and legs were burning up. They were so hot that it literally burnt my hand. All of my mother's life, her feet were cold.

I went to the nursing station to tell the nurse, and she replied to me, "The room is hot. That's all."

I asked her to come into my mother's room and feel her feet and legs. The nurse couldn't believe how hot her feet and legs were and confirmed that something was really wrong. She put in a call for a doctor to see my mother, and it ended up that my mother had an infection in her body.

Another time when I went to visit my mom, she didn't look right. I asked her if she felt sick. She let out a loud sigh and turned her head away from me.

I then proceeded to work my way with my fingers from her chest cavity, and down her stomach. I noticed that she flinched and went to get the nurse.

The nurse checked all of my mother's vitals and said that she was okay, that it was just the Alzheimer's. As the nurse walked out of my

49

mother's room, my mother threw up all over herself, her blankets, and her sheets.

The nurse was baffled and asked me, "How did you know that your mother was sick?"

I responded, "She told me."

She asked, "But she can't talk, how could she tell you?"

I just said, "She told me."

From being with my mother all day and night, I was able to read my mother's eyes and facial expressions.

After one and a half years working for the county part time, they hired me in a full-time position with them in the Child Support Paternity department. I was happy and sad at the same time.

I was happy, because there were insufficient funds in my checking account. My overdraft was $3,000, but I was fortunate to have overdraft protection. Plus, my MasterCard bill was over $5,000, with accumulating interest rates on both accounts.

Now that I was working full time, my hours were 8:30 a.m. to 4:30 p.m., so my mother had to have an aid feed her breakfast, lunch, and dinner. I know that the aid wasn't feeding her all of her

50

food, because it took me a half hour every day to feed my mother, and the feeders sometimes had three to four patients to feed within a short time span, so I know my mother wasn't get enough time to be fed her dinner.

I came to a conclusion and told the nurse to leave the hot lid on my mother's dinner. I told her that I would feed her when I arrived. They ate dinner at 4:30, and I would arrive there by 5:00. That worked out so much better for me and my mother's schedule.

Now I was content to work full time. I would go to work, then to the nursing home, feed my mother, change her, change her sheets if needed, and make sure that she took her medications before I left. The doctor also prescribed Lorazepam (Ativan), for my mom's anxiety.

CAREGIVER'S TIP

My mother's right hand became deformed, and her nails started digging into her hand. I asked the nurse what I could do to prevent my mother's nails from cutting into her hand, and she told me they could order a Posey terry cloth covered palm cone. That was the perfect solution.

Patti Bonczkowski

CHAPTER 9

Abiding By Mom's Living Will

One day when I arrived at the nursing home after work, I was called over by the nurses and the head nurse. They told me, "Your mother's weight is down to 80 pounds. Do you want to honor her Living Will?"

I told them, "My mother does not want feeding tubes or anything else to keep her alive."

The head nurse said, "We understand. We just wanted to make sure that you comprehended the Living Will and what it means exactly."

The nurses went on to explain to me that it meant if my mother gets pneumonia, they will not send her to a hospital, and if she has a heart attack, they will not revive her.

My mom and I were extremely close, and I couldn't imagine just allowing her to die in front of my face, knowing that she could be saved. I told them that I had to sleep on it and give my response when I came from work the following day.

That night I thought about my mom's Living Will, and that it was the best decision for HER. My mom no longer fed herself, was on thickened liquids to prevent aspiration pneumonia, and couldn't use the toilet, walk, or talk. She only had a blank stare. What kind of life was she living? Besides, these were her wishes - not mine, even though I did agree with her.

I realized it was in my mother's best interest to let go and let God do the rest. If I prolonged her life, that would mean that she'd just lie there for the remaining of her so-called life.

The following morning after work, I went down to the nursing home to fill out paperwork for Hospice. That was the BEST decision that I made. They gave my mother a brand-new bed and mattress, and a recliner wheelchair. They told me that I could give my mother pain killers anytime I thought she needed them and that I did not have to wait every three to four hours anymore, and if a nurse said the doctor's orders are every four hours, I just had to call Hospice and they'd call the nurses' station. My mom was no longer under doctor's care.

My mother eventually got bed sores from not being able to move around. Bed sores develop when the blood supply to skin is cut off for 2-3 hours. The skin dies, and the bed sores turn red and painful.

The nurses and nurse's aides – including myself, would turn my mother on one side for a while, then turn her to the other side, and we'd also apply a prescription cream to her sores.

I arrived at the nursing home after work and saw that the feeder was putting too much food in my mother's mouth, and she was refusing it. My mother would only allow me to put 1/4 forkful in her mouth at a time.

Finally, I figured out that's why she was losing weight, because she wouldn't eat if the feeder put more than 1/4 forkful in her mouth. I spoke with the head nurse and asked if they could try to give her less food on the fork when they fed her. They listened to me, and my mother gained some weight back.

There were times when my mother only ate ice cream. The doctor said not to worry, because Alzheimer's patients love their sweets and that would help her gain weight.

My mom was on Hospice care for three years. She was also fortunate to have this one awesome aid, Gerard. He always explained everything to my mother before he did it. He'd say, "Miss Barbara, I'm going to stand you up, I'm now going to sit you down on the bed, I'm going to place your legs on the bed, and I'm going to lower you down onto your pillow."

My mother loved Gerard. After Gerard would leave the room, I'd ask my mother if she liked Gerard, and then she'd smile.

My mother had a few awesome nurses too: There was Gloria, John, and a couple others that I wish I remembered their names. They were exceptional nurses.

Two days before my mother passed away, I went to feed her, and she clamped her lips shut. I knew this meant the end was near.

I ran hysterically to the head nurse Gloria, explaining that my mother wasn't eating. Gloria was a sweetheart. She reminded me that my mom loved ice cream. Yep, Gloria was correct – I was so relieved to see my mother eat.

Letting go of someone you love is very hard to do. My mom was my mother, my best friend, and now like a child to me. I couldn't bear to see her die.

The following day, I had to go over my mother's Living Will again. She wasn't doing well. Afterwards, I proceeded to my mother's room #322. As I fed my mom lunch, I noticed something on my mom's bib. I brought it to the nurse to see what it was. A tooth had fallen out. A little later, another tooth fell out.

CAREGIVER'S TIP

Bed sores develop when the blood supply to skin is cut off for 2-34 hours. The skin dries, and the sores turn red and painful. When my mother developed bed sores, the nurses and nurse's aides – including myself, would turn my mother on one side for a while, then turn her to the other side, and we'd also apply a prescription cream to her sores.

Patti Bonczkowski

CHAPTER 10

Held By My Mother's Angel Wings

That night at dinner, once again my mother clamped her lips tight and that's when I knew, we were at the end. I called Hospice and told them that I didn't think that she'd make it through the night.

I was right. The nursing home called me at 7:00 a.m. and told me that my mother wasn't going to make it much longer.

I rushed down there at 7:00 a.m. and slept next to my mother in her bed at the nursing home until she passed away at 1:50 a.m.

Before my mom passed, her breathing became very rapid. I asked the nurse to come to my mom's room because I couldn't keep up with her breathing. The nurse said that she was in distress and administered morphine to calm her breathing down.

Hospice instructed me to have the nurses give my mother morphine whenever I felt that she needed it, because my mom was under their care.

While my mother laid there dying, I told her that her parents, sister, nephew and my father were waiting for her. They were going to have a huge party the second that she arrived. I was saying that while tears were pouring down my face.

I also told her, that she'd have to leave in order for another baby to be born, and that she didn't have to worry about me, that I was fine. I asked my mother to please wrap her angel arms around me when she left this world. Crying silent tears, I asked her to promise me that she would.

I remember that I had to go to the bathroom around 7:30 p.m. I know that your loved ones usually pass away when you walk out the door.

My mom's bathroom was in her room, and I told her that she was in the room when I was born, and that I wanted to be there when she passed away. I went to the bathroom, leaving the door opened so that I could see her. Thank God, she listened to me. You know how you've heard, how your deceased loved ones come to meet you to bring you home? Well, my mother wasn't able to turn her head for months. All of a sudden, she looked around at every corner of the ceiling staring at something. I asked her was it my father, her sister, nephew or her parents, but she just kept moving her head and scanning the entire ceiling. I guess that everyone came to bring her home.

I kept watching my mother's legs for mottling. Mottling is a blotchy, red-purplish marbling of the skin. It frequently occurs first on the feet, and then travels up the legs. Mottling of the skin before death is common and occurs during the final week of life. Usually, when it gets halfway up the legs, or a little more, is when they pass.

My mother never had that gurgling sound that I've heard some people speak about when their loved ones passed away.

While I was lying next to my mom, holding her close in my arms, she stopped breathing. I buzzed for the nurse to come into her room, but when they came in, she began breathing again.

About five minutes later, my mom stopped breathing again just as the nurse came in with her morphine. This time it was for good. She did not gasp for air. My mom went peacefully.

I then removed the oxygen from her nose, gave her a kiss and told her that I loved her.

The nurse that was on duty when my mom passed, I've never seen before because she was on a later shift. For some reason, she asked me to help her close my mother's eyes!!! She told me that the funeral directors don't like the eyes open.

Here I was, trying to close my mother's eyes, and they were frozen open. Then the nurse told me to call the funeral home at 1:50 a.m.

I said. "You want ME to call them?"

And she responded, "Yes."

I said, "What am I supposed to tell them at 1:50 a.m.???"

She told me to ask if they were going to pick my mom up now or should the nursing home place her in the morgue!!!

I was in shock but did as she asked. I knew that it wasn't my place to be closing my mother's eyes OR calling the funeral home!!!

After calling the MORGUE, I went in to clean my mother's room out. A week prior to her passing, I had bought her new hospital gowns. While I was walking to the nurses' station, to tell her to please donate them to any of the patients who could use them, my mother's wings wrapped around my body holding me close. My mom remembered.

After my mother left the physical world – I can't really explain what happened to me. The only thing that I remember was that I kissed my mom, told her that I loved her, and then just proceeded to clean her room out, while my mom was still lying there.

I don't remember going back to say goodbye one last time, or even leaving the nursing home. I think that after my mom's wings held me, I knew she went home and that my mother was going to be fine.

I had a beautiful spiritual service for my mother. I wrote her eulogy, hired a singer to sing: *How do I Live Without You, I Believe* by Diamond Rio and *Penny's from Heaven.*

I didn't think that I'd be able to read the eulogy, so I had Reverend Carole Boyce do the honors.

I asked the singer to sing: *How Do I Live Without You* **MOM?**

The last song was *Penny's from Heaven* (because that was my mom's maiden name, and she also used it for her first name).

I Believe (by Diamond Rio)

Every now and then,
Soft as breath upon my skin,
I feel you come back again.

And it's like you haven't been,
Gone a moment from my side.
Like the tears were never cried,
Like the hands of time are holding you and me.

And with all my heart I'm sure,
We're closer than we ever were.
I don't have to hear or see,
I've got all the proof I need.
There are more than angels watching over me.
I believe, oh I believe.

Now when you die your life goes on,
It doesn't end here when you're gone.
Every soul is filled with light,
It never ends and if I'm right.
Our love can even reach across eternity,
I believe, oh I believe.

Forever, you're a part of me.
Forever, in the heart of me.
I will hold you even longer if I can.
Oh the people who don't see the most,
See that I believe in ghosts.
And if that makes me crazy, then I am
'Cause I believe

Oh, I believe
There are more than angels watching over me.
I believe, oh I believe.
Every now and then,
Soft as breath upon my skin,
I feel you come back again.
And I believe.

64

CHAPTER 11

Reflections Of Love For My Mom

I wrote my mom's eulogy for her service and wanted to share it with you in this book.

Eulogy That I Wrote For My Mom

I'm here to share some stories with all of you about my mother and the joy she brought to our family and to everyone in this room whose life she touched.

Here are some fond memories of my mother, that I'd like to share with you:

We all thought that our mother should have written books, because every time she told someone a story, she kept changing it to make it better and better. We could have been sitting on the porch all day, but each time she retold the story she revised to make it seem as if we had been to the amusement park or Paris. She was never one to make a conversation boring.

I remember the time that my mother used Zip Strip to take the paint off of the stairs, and her hands got all swollen, and I had to take her to the hospital. I said, "Mom, why didn't you put gloves on first?" and she responded, "I did" and showed them to me - they weren't rubber gloves. They were extra absorbent ones. Swollen hands and all, my mother was still cooking, until I walked in the door and brought her to the emergency room. In the worst situations she still made us laugh at the funny things that she did. Her laughter brought so much joy into our lives and made us laugh along with her.

My mother LOVED the holidays. She always changed all of the curtains in every room for each holiday and decorated heavily, and made the house look so beautiful when she was finished. She made each and every holiday so special, not only for me but for everyone.

My cousin Ricky, who she's probably having a ball with right now, used to bring his guitar and she couldn't wait to sing along. She made all of us laugh because she sounded just like Edith Bunker on *All In The Family* when she sang, but she didn't care. She sang her heart out anyway which made our day even brighter.

We all have so many special memories: Trips to amusement parks, swimming, going to tricky trays, visiting with her sisters Paula and Candy, going out places with her sister-in-law Ceil and her niece Jan, and going out with her Buddy Annette.

The list just goes on and on, because she loved life and was a LOT of fun to be around. She was always a kid at heart.

Every time that our old neighborhood on East 31st St in Paterson gets together, the stories are always about my mother and father and the fun that we used to have at our house.

Back then I took everything that my parents gave to us for granted, but now when I look back, I appreciate everything my parents did for us.

My mother always made her children and her goddaughter, Linda (Landi) Vassilatos) matching ice skating outfits, Halloween costumes and clothes. She even made two of my dogs their costumes for Halloween.

My mother was so creative and talented. I wish that I would have inherited *some* of her skills.

Mom loved spending time with her sister-in-law Ceil, going to craft fairs and eating out. They were so very close. Naturally, wherever my aunt Ceil and Mom went, her niece Jan was right there making sure that the both of them didn't get into trouble.

I have to share a story about my mother bringing her baby chicks to work to show her co-workers just how cute they were, and when she opened the box in back of her car on her break, they were all dead, because she forgot to make holes in the box and leave the window opened a little. She told us that she was never so embarrassed in her entire life. She laughed as she told the story though.

I remember when Mom was asked to watch her aunt Betty's dog for her, and my mother let it out in her backyard and it never came back, so my mother talked her aunt into getting a cat. My mother told us that she felt bad, but couldn't stop laughing.

My mother even asked me if she could watch her grand-dog Precious – I don't think so!

My mother's eyes used to pop out of her head when she saw a Garage Sale - I always had to speed up, so that I didn't have to stop at one, but if I had to do it over again, I'd stop at each and every one of them, no matter how much junk the person had on their lawn.

Mom loved doing arts and crafts and so much more. I remember the time she stayed at my apartment. My mother was so bored that she decided to paint things that I didn't want painted with polka dots or whatever, and I got upset at her. What I'd do to have her paint ANYTHING she wanted, however she wanted right now, and I know that I'd love the end results because SHE did it.

Now, I'd like to acknowledge a VERY special person in this room. Her name is Annette Austin, who met my mother years ago at work. She has been my mother's BEST buddy since and became a member of our family.

When my mother got to the point where she wasn't able to communicate anymore, for some reason my mother remembered to say, "I love Annette." I'd say, "Don't you love me Mommy?" and she'd reply, "No, I love my Buddy Annette." Everybody used to hate hearing my mother talk about Annette. Everything was, *Annette and I did this,* or *Annette likes to do anything I like to do. I just love Annette, Annette, Annette, Annette.*

69

We didn't even know poor Annette and were complaining about her. Then once we met Annette, we instantly knew why my mother loved her so much. Annette, there's no escaping us now – you're stuck with us.

Mom, we'll all remember your smile, laughter and the sunshine you brought into our lives. You were and are our world, our rock, our mother, and the BEST friend a daughter could ever have, and now you're our Guardian Angel.

I thank God that I believe that life continues, because there would be a terrible void in our lives if we didn't feel her presence anymore. Although we will always miss our mother, her spiritual presence will always be with us.

My mother always said, "I love you to pieces," and Mom we all love you to pieces too. I'll always be your "Patti-Cake." Rest in peace with the angels.

CHAPTER 12

My Alzheimer's Donation Page

I miss my mom and the times that we spent at her sisters' houses in PA, swimming at The Spa, walking around the park, grabbing a bite to eat, and just enjoying life together.

She had an awesome hearty laugh, and I used to love spending EVERY moment with her. Then one day, my mom laughed no more. There were no more conversations with her, because she couldn't respond. She even lost the ability to use her hands and pick up her utensils or a cup.

As her Alzheimer's advanced, she had to be fed and taken care of 24/7.

When I went to the nursing home straight from work, I changed and fed my Mom, took her out for walks in her wheelchair, watched TV and ate dinner with her and stayed with her until she fell fast asleep.

I looked deep into her eyes and could tell she wanted to speak to me but couldn't.

My mom was confined to a bed, no longer able to get up and walk about. She used to laugh and clap her hands when she saw me walk through the door on her floor of the nursing home, then that even ended.

Towards the end of my mother's precious life, her brain shrunk drastically due to nerve cell death and tissue loss, which made her fingers clench and made her nails dig into her hands. We also had to give her thickened liquids and meals, to prevent aspiration pneumonia.

The last 19 hours of my mom's life, I slept by her side never leaving her alone, until the angels took her home.

There was NO magic pill that would have returned my mom to us, and I, and the rest of the family, miss her EVERY single day. It scared me to watch what had happened to her, because I wonder and fear if this too will be my fate.

We need to find a cure for Alzheimer's. It is a terrible disease, and I felt so helpless that I wasn't able to save my mother.

I love and miss my mom EVERY second of every day! I'm so sorry, that they didn't find a cure for my mom before she was taken away from me.

Kisses and hugs to my mom in heaven.

Alzheimer's disease has **NO survivors**. It destroys brain cells and causes memory changes, erratic behaviors, and loss of body functions. It slowly **and PAINFULLY** takes away a person's identity, ability to connect with others, think, eat, walk, and find their way home.

It is SO DIFFICULT to watch somebody that you love lose their memory, independence, and ultimately their life – to Alzheimer's.

It's our nation's MOST expensive disease; it is the leading cause of death in the US without ANY known prevention, treatments or cure.

Alzheimer's kills more than Breast AND Prostate Cancer COMBINED!!!!

Please **HELP** donate towards a good cause. Our vision is a world without Alzheimer's.

P.S. A LOT of us have already lost one or MORE people that we've loved to this cruel disease. But with your donations, hopefully they'll find a cure, so that nobody has to suffer with Alzheimer's anymore.

Thank you so much again, for ALL of your support and donations.

In loving Memory of My Mother, Barbara (Penny) Bonczkowski

I had to mention one last thing. From spending unlimited hours per day at the nursing home, I became friends with other caregivers. So one day after my mom had passed, I went to the nursing home to visit and stood near my mother's room #322. Some lady came out of the room from visiting with her dad and told me that she saw a woman one night in there. My mother was the last person in that room, so I'm guessing that it could have been her.

CAREGIVER'S TIP

Alzheimer's destroys brain cells and causes memory changes, erratic behaviors, and loss of body functions. It slowly and PAINFULLY takes away a person's identity, ability to connect with others, think, eat, walk, and find their way home.

Patti Bonczkowski

CHAPTER 13

Tips And Tools To Make Your Life Easier

- ➢ Adult bibs
- ➢ Velcro sneakers
- ➢ Pants with elastic waist
- ➢ Swivel chair pad
- ➢ Hospital gowns with opening in the back
- ➢ Adult Depends
- ➢ Straws
- ➢ CD player (play songs they used to like, kiddie songs and Christmas songs or songs from their era)
- ➢ Guard rail for tub or shower
- ➢ Raised toilet seat
- ➢ Washable bed pads (to protect couch and bedding)
- ➢ The 36-Hour Day Book (by Nancy Mace)
- ➢ Non slip socksNon slip tub mat or stickers for inside of shower/tub

- Long mural to cover door and doorknob, so they don't think that there's a door there, and start to roam outside.

- Remove knobs off of the stove, so they don't turn them on and start a fire.

- Remove spark plugs without their knowledge in their vehicle, so they think that the car doesn't work. Otherwise, they'll go for a ride and get lost.

- They say placing a large black rug by the door SHOULD prevent them for going outside. Supposedly, when Alzheimer's patients see a black rug, they think that it's a hole in the floor.
(My Mother never wandered, so I'm not sure if the mural or the black rug works, but it's worth a try).

- Never lift a person up by their arm – You could pull their arm out of the socket. ALWAYS place your hand under their armpit, then lift them up.

➢ Do NOT get the "Fallen and I Can't Get Up" - They can't comprehend how to use it.

➢ If your loved one wanders outside of the house, then get a tracking device. Most people with Alzheimer's who wander end up lost and sometimes die outside in the cold, the excessive heat or get hit by a vehicle.

1. **AngelSense**

AngelSense provides caregivers a comprehensive view of their loved one's activities, comings, and goings. The device attaches to a loved one's clothing and can only be removed by the caregiver. It provides a daily timeline of locations, routes and transit speed and sends an instant alert to caregivers if their loved one is in an unfamiliar place. Caregivers can listen in to hear what is happening around their loved one, can receive an alert if their loved one has not left for an appointment on time, allows caregivers to communicate with their loved one, and sends an alarm to locate your loved one – wherever they are.

2. GPS Smart Sole

Similar to the GPS Shoe and from the same designers, the GPS Smart Sole fits into most shoes and allows caregivers to track their loved one from any smartphone, tablet or web browser. The shoe insert is enabled with GPS technology and allows real-time syncing, a detailed report of location history, and allows users to set up a safe radius for their loved one.

3. iTraq

iTraq is a tracking device that can be used to track pretty much anything – from loved ones to luggage, this tracker pairs with an app on a smartphone to find anyone and anything. For seniors, the device includes a motion or fall sensor and will send an alert if a fall is detected. It also has a temperature sensor. Their newest device, the iTraq Nano is marketed as the world's smallest all-in-one tracking device that has global tracking, two months battery life, is water and dust resistant is able to be charged wirelessly. The device also has an SOS button that will send an instant alert to friends and family, notifying them of their loved one's precise location.

4. MedicAlert Safely Home

This device was originally created to help emergency responders treat patients who could not speak for themselves. Today, the device also helps people with dementia who wander. The device is worn as a bracelet and when a loved one goes missing, caregivers can call the police and have the police call the 24-hour hotline to get the location of the missing person. Caregivers can also call the hotline themselves to get information. In addition to a tracking device, the bracelet has important medical information engraved upon it.

5. Mindme

Mindme offers two lifesaving devices, one is a location device, the other is an alarm. The alarm allows the user to alert a Mindme response center in case of a fall or other emergency. The locator device is specifically designed for people with dementia or other cognitive disabilities. The simple device works as a pendant that can be put in a bag or pocket and allows caregivers to track the user online at any time. Caregivers can also set a radius for the user and will be alerted if the person travels outside that zone.

6. PocketFinder

PocketFinder was founded in 2005 by a single parent who wanted to know the whereabouts of his young son, especially when he wasn't there. Their slogan, "If you love it, locate it!" sums up their philosophy and service offerings. Tracking everything from luggage to pets to children to seniors, the company offers **a wide range of emerging technological products**. PocketFinder is designed to be the smallest tracker on the market and the device can fit in the palm of your hand. It has a battery life up to one week and allows caregivers to track wearers through a user-friendly app. The device was updated in January 2017 and now includes three location technologies including GPS, Cell ID and Google Wi-Fi Touch. It also now has an SOS button.

7. Project Lifesaver

The mission of Project Lifesaver is "to provide timely response to save lives and reduce potential injury for adults and children who wander due to

Alzheimer's, autism and other related condition or disorders." Seniors who are enrolled in Project Lifesaver are given a personal transmitter that they wear around their ankle. If they wander, the caregiver calls a local Project Lifesaver agency and a trained team will respond. Recovery times average 30 minutes and many who wander are found within a few miles of their home. In addition to the location device, Project Lifesaver works with public safety agencies to train them on the risks associated with wandering.

8. Revolutionary Tracker

Revolutionary Tracker has location-based systems to keep tabs on seniors who may wander. The company strives to "bring an unparalleled level of functionality, capability, ease of use and relevant presentation of information to give people the ability to extend communication, knowledge, protection and care for their loved ones." Their GPS enabled personal tracker features an SOS button for emergencies and offers real-time tracking. This device allows multiple seniors to be tracked at the same time and syncs directly to a caregiver's smart phone or computer.

9. <u>Safe Link</u>

Safe Link is another GPS tracking system available for people with Alzheimer's or dementia. The product promises to "increase safety for the elderly, promote independent living and ultimately lead to a healthier lifestyle." Safe Link is a small device carried by the person who may wander. The device periodically sends its geographic coordinates to central servers and family members and caregivers can view the wearer's location via website. The device needs to be charged and worn at all times. All devices have an SOS button for emergencies.

10. <u>Trax</u>

Trax is touted as the world's smallest and lightest live GPS tracker. The device sends position, speed, and direction through the cellular network directly to your app on a smartphone. Trax comes with a clip that is easy to attach to a loved one. The app allows caregivers to set "Geofences" and will send an alert if a loved one enters or leaves a predetermined area. Trax Geofences have no size limit, caregivers can create as many fence areas as needed, and can schedule when those virtual fences are in effect.

Alzheimer's Poem

Do not ask me to remember,
Do not try to make me understand.
Let me rest and know you're with me,
Kiss my cheek and hold my hand.
I'm confused beyond your concept,
I am sad and sick and lost.
All I know is that I need you with me,
To be with me at all cost.
Do not lose your patience with me,
Do not curse or scold or cry.
I can't help the way I'm acting,
Can't be different though I try.
Just remember that I need you,
The best of me is gone.
Please don't fail to stand beside me,
Love me until my life is done.

(Owen Darnell)

CHAPTER 14

Pictures From Our Journey

My sign that I made for my Alzheimer's Walks

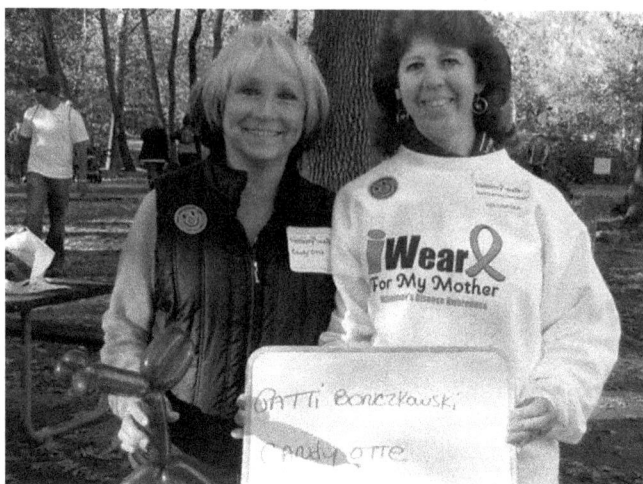

My mother's sister, Candy Otte and myself at Alzheimer's Walk

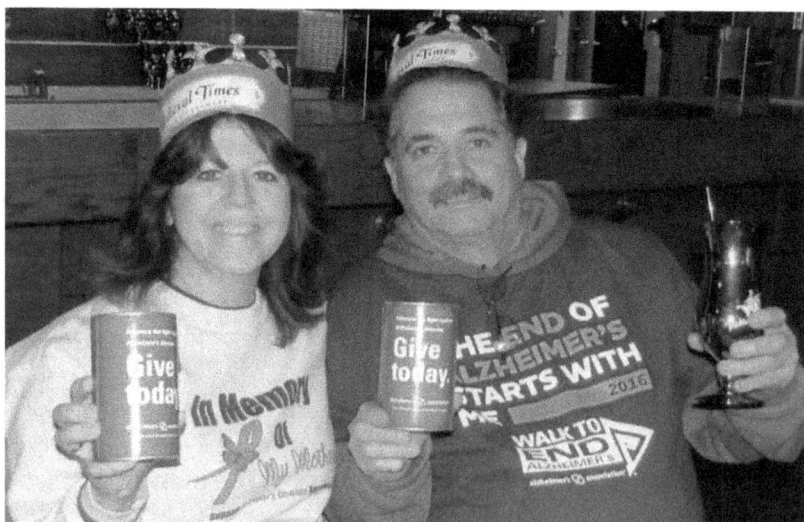

Myself with my significant other, Anthony Paletto at an Alzheimer's Appreciation Dinner, for money that we've raised.

Myself at Alzheimer's Walk

**Myself with my mother's sister, Candy Otte
at Alzheimer's Walk**

Pin that I made for My Alzheimer's Walks

My mom, Barbara (Penny) Bonczkowski, in Advanced stages of Alzheimer's

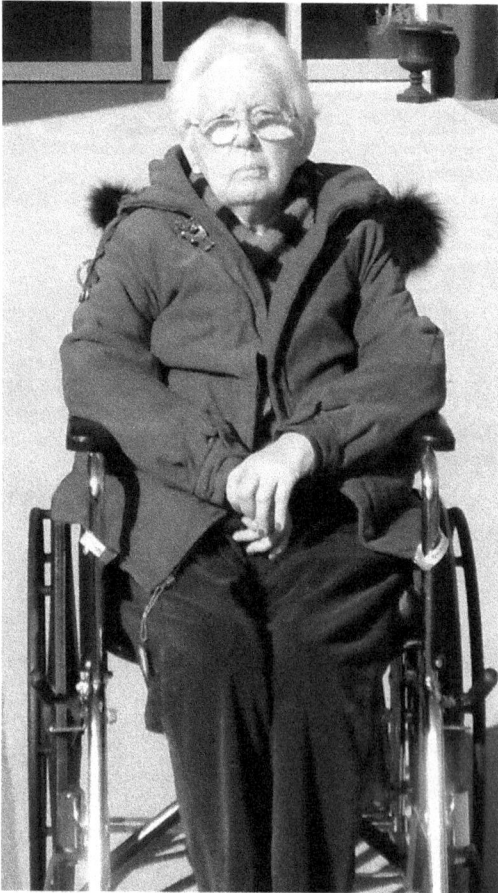

**My significant other Anthony Paletto,
showing support for Alzheimer's**

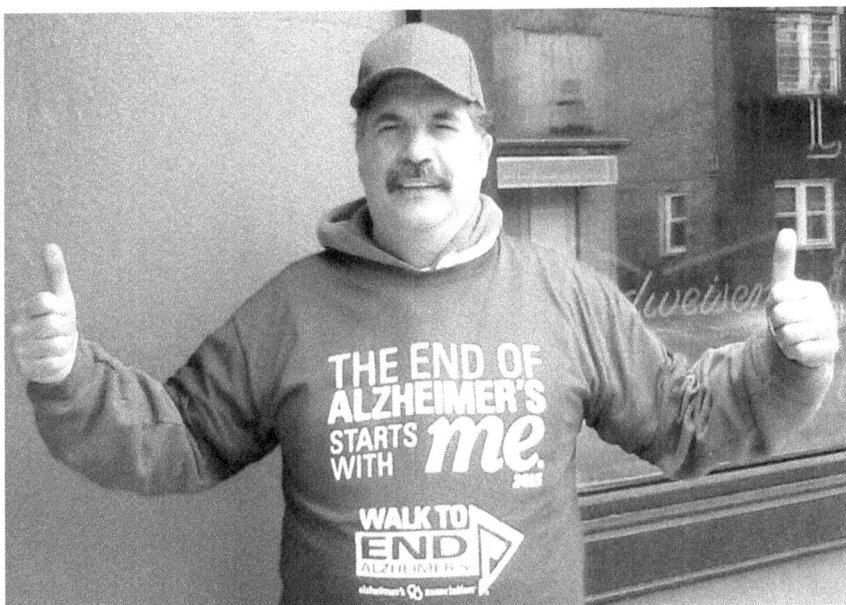

My mom Barbara Penny Bonczkowski, in Advanced Stages of Alzheimer's

My mother Barbara (Penny) Bonczkowski, before Alzheimer's disease

Patti Bonczkowski now

In Loving Memory of

BARBARA L. BONCZKOWSKI
August 28, 2013

We sat beside your bedside,
Our hearts were crushed and sore;
We did our best to the end,
Til we could do no more.
In tears we watched you sinking,
We watched you fade away;
And though our hearts were breaking,
We knew you could not stay.
You left behind some aching hearts -
That loved you most sincere;
We never shall and never will
Forget you Mother dear.

ABOUT THE AUTHOR

Patti **Bonczkowski** has been doing the walks for Alzheimer's for the past 11-years or longer. She was a caregiver to her mother for 10 years with more hands on for the last 6-years of her precious life.

Patti has also volunteered, for 5 years with the American Red Cross Disaster Team, on a national level. Patti was a shelter manager, drove the emergency response vehicle to do mass feedings **_and delivered_** clean-up supplies. She was also a team leader when she responded to fires.

Patti has also volunteered for the past 6 years for Babe Ruth Baseball in Little Ferry, NJ, as a team administrator. She has also taken pictures of all of the kids playing baseball, and made baseball yearbooks for the Red Bird team, where her significant other Anthony Paletto coached.

ORDER INFORMATION

You can order autographed copies of
Alzheimer's, My Mother, And Me by emailing the
author directly using the email address below.

Patti Bonczkowski

Email Address:

pattibonczkowski@yahoo.com

Books are available at Amazon.com, BN.com,
Kindle and Your Local Bookstores (By Request)

Please leave a review for this book on Amazon and let other readers know how much you enjoyed reading it.

Thank you!

www.ingramcontent.com/pod-product-compliance
Lightning Source LLC
Chambersburg PA
CBHW060552100426
42742CB00013B/2527